Quinn
and the
Worry Channel

A story about mindfulness, worry and sleep

Written and illustrated by Linda Ryden

Dedication

To my dearest friend Cheryl who gave me a bunny when I really needed one.

To Quinn, a brave and kind person who really wanted to be in this book.

And many thanks to The Healthier, Greener, Kinder Foundation for their generous support of the production of this book!

https://healthiergreenerkinder.org/

"Good night, Quinn!" said Dad. "You've had a busy day. Time to get some sleep. Love you!"

"Love you, too!" said Quinn.

"Okay Fred the Bunny," said Quinn. "Time for bed! Good night!"

Quinn and Fred cuddled up, but Quinn couldn't settle down.

"Ugh!" said Quinn.

"I can't get comfortable.
I can't fall asleep!
Ugh!"

"Oh my goodness! Stop flopping around!" said Fred the Bunny. "I can't get any sleep with you tossing and turning like that!"

Quinn jumped and stared at Fred.

"Fred the Bunny?!" said Quinn.

"You can talk?"

Fred the Bunny said, "Of course! I can talk... when I want to...."

"Gee, I'm sorry. I just can't sleep." said Quinn sadly.

"Why not?" asked Fred. "You were so tired during dinner that you fell asleep in your mashed potatoes!"

Quinn said, "Yeah that was embarrassing. I don't know. I was really tired before, but now I can't sleep. My mind can't stop thinking."

"What are you thinking about?" asked Fred.

"Well... we have a math test tomorrow, I think my friend Mason is mad at me, I left my backpack on the playground, my basketball team is playing in the championships this weekend, and...."

"Whoa! Hold on there," said Fred. "It sounds like your mind is stuck on **The Worry Channel**."

"What?" said Quinn. "What's **The Worry Channel**?"

"Imagine that you have a remote control device in your mind," said Fred.

"Like the one we use to change the channels on the tv?" asked Quinn.

"Yes, like that," said Fred. "All day long you choose different channels. Like the **Listen to the Teacher Channel** or the **Dribble the Basketball Channel** or the **Play the Guitar Channel** or the **Ride on a Dragon Channel**."

"Wait, what?! Ride on a dragon?!" said Quinn looking shocked.

"Well... I don't know what you do all day," laughed Fred. "I'm always stuck here in your room!" Quinn laughed too.

"Sometimes," Fred continued, "you choose a channel and your mind stays focused on one thing at a time. But sometimes your mind changes the channel without you even noticing!"

"What?! How does that work?" asked Quinn.

"Well," explained Fred, "have you ever noticed that sometimes you are listening carefully to your teacher telling you what the homework is going to be, and then your stomach starts grumbling, and then all you can think about is lunch? Then your teacher says, 'Okay, that's the homework!' and you have no idea what they said?"

Quinn said, "Oh yeah, that has definitely happened to me."

"So," said Fred, "sometimes our mind just changes the channel without asking us. It's like your mind is in charge of you instead of you being in charge of your mind!"

"Whoa that's wild!" said Quinn. "But what does this have to do with sleeping?"

"Sometimes when you are going to sleep your mind decides that it's a great time to watch **The Worry Channel**," said Fred.

"What kinds of things are on **The Worry Channel**?" asked Quinn.

"Shows like **Am I Going to Fail the Math Test?** or **Is My Backpack Going to Get All Wet?** or **Is Mason Mad at Me?** or **What if We Lose the Championship?**" answered Fred.

"Oh, you mean those kinds of thoughts are called worries?" asked Quinn.

"Exactly!" said Fred. "And **The Worry Channel** is no fun to watch."

"I've never heard any of my friends talk about **The Worry Channel**," said Quinn sadly. "I'm probably the only one with this problem."

"Oh no," said Fred. "Almost everybody watches **The Worry Channel** sometimes. Most people worry, but nobody really wants to."

Fred asked, "Would you ever invite Mason over for a playdate and say, "Hey! I've got a great idea. Let's sit here and imagine bad things happening to us!"

Quinn said, "What?! No! That would be crazy! I would never do that."

"That's right," said Fred. "And you don't lie down in bed at night and say, 'Okay now that I'm all comfy and cozy, let's turn on that **Worry Channel** and think about lots of bad things that could happen.'"

"Hmmm…." said Quinn. "You're right. I don't really plan to do that. It just happens."

"Of course you don't!" said Fred smiling. "But the good news is you can actually learn how to help your mind choose what to focus on when it does happen. Then you can take a break from worrying and get a good night's sleep."

"Really?" said Quinn. "That would be great. But how can I change the channel to something better?"

"Well," said Fred, "that takes a little practice. The first step is just noticing that your mind is watching **The Worry Channel**."

"How do I do that?" asked Quinn.

"One way to practice," said Fred, "is to focus your mind on one thing and then try to notice when your mind starts doing something else, or changing the channel."

"Okay…" said Quinn, feeling a little confused.

"So let's choose something to focus on," said Fred. "When I do it, I like to focus on my breath. I count my breaths one at a time."

"Count my breaths?" asked Quinn looking puzzled.

"Yes," said Fred. "Imagine that you are setting your remote control to **The Counting Breaths Channel**. Then every time you breathe in and out you count it."

"Okay." said Quinn. "I'll give it a try!"

"Good!" said Fred. "Grab your imaginary remote control device. Then, just start counting your breaths, and every time you notice that your mind has changed the channel, just click your remote control and change it back to **The Counting Breaths Channel**. Ready?"

Quinn said, "I think so."

"You might want to close your eyes or look down into your lap," suggested Fred. Quinn started counting, breathing in and out slowly.

"Wait! Now I'm on the **Ice Cream Channel!**" said Quinn. "That's okay," said Fred. "Just try to change back to **The Counting Breaths Channel.**"

"Okay, I'll try again," said Quinn.

"Oh no! Now I'm on the **Math Test Channel**!" said Quinn.

"Okay so just try to change it back." reminded Fred.

Quinn kept trying. "This is kind of hard. But also kind of fun!"

"The more you practice this the easier it gets," said Fred. He added, "If counting your breaths doesn't feel comfortable, you could focus on a sound like the refrigerator humming instead. Whatever works for you is fine. It feels good to be able to decide what channel you want to be watching."

"Next time you're worried," Fred suggested, "you can change the channel to **The Stuff I'm Great at Channel**.

Or the **Are Narwhals Real Channel?**

Or the **What if the World Were Made of Marshmallows Channel!**"

"That sounds fun!" said Quinn smiling.

"It is!" said Fred. "Being able to decide what you want your mind to be doing is kind of a super power."

"A super power?!" said Quinn. "That's awesome!!"

"Remember," said Fred, "this takes practice, but once you get the hang of it, it can really help. Do you think you're ready to go to sleep now? You can watch the **Getting Some Zzzzs Channel**...."

Quinn yawned and said, "Thanks Fred! I think I know what channel I want to watch now.

Good night!"

A Note From The Author

I have always struggled with falling asleep. The minute the lights went off, my mind would start to race with all the "what ifs". I didn't just worry at bedtime, I worried constantly. When I started to practice mindfulness and discovered that I could learn how to pay attention to my thoughts and actually change or redirect them it was a life changer. How I wish that I had these metacognition skills when I was a little kid!

Understanding that I have some control over what my mind is doing has made it much easier for me to recognize when my mind is worrying and deliberately try to think about something else. This ability also helps me focus on my work or on people who are talking to me or even on just enjoying a pleasant moment. My Peace Class students at Lafayette Elementary School in Washington, D.C. love learning about what we call Remote Control Breathing. We sit and we pay attention to and count our breaths and we try to notice whenever we aren't counting breaths anymore. Then we try to label whatever our mind was doing. Using the metaphor of the remote control in your mind changing the channel seems to work really well for my students.

I hope that you and the kids in your life will enjoy this little story and that it will help you all get a little more sleep.

In peace,

Linda

Linda Ryden is the author of the Henry and Friends storybook series, and the Peace of Mind Curriculum Series. She is the full-time Peace Teacher at Lafayette Elementary School and the founder and co-director of Peace of Mind, Inc., a nonprofit organization dedicated to developing and sharing resources that support teaching mindfulness, kindness, conflict resolution and social justice in our schools.

Kids and Worry
Rosemary Cohen, LSW

It is very common for kids to deal with worry, anxiety, and trouble with sleep. Especially in the age of a global pandemic, gun violence in schools, and climate change, children have the weight of the world on their shoulders. The metacognition exercises in this book are some of the best tools for children (and adults) to better manage feelings of worry.

For anxious kids and chronic worriers, it may be helpful to hear that anxiety can be a bit of a superpower. Anxiety is a survival skill that humans have employed since the beginning of time and keeps us safe in dangerous situations. Anxiety is a fear response that lets us know when we need to take action to stay safe, like when we need to go inside during a thunderstorm. However, we know that the superpowers of anxiety can sometimes work too hard to keep us safe, and they end up making our lives more difficult. Anxiety can make it difficult or impossible to sleep, focus, or even make it through the school day. This book shows that by using metacognition, you can work on keeping anxiety and worries at bay when they are no longer useful feelings. Metacognition can ground us in reality and remind us that we are safe and no longer need to be using anxiety as a survival tool.

Metacognition is an excellent tool to manage anxiety, but it is important to seek professional help if your child is experiencing severe anxiety or depression.

We are very grateful to clinical psychologist Laura Hayes, PhD, Rosemary Cohen, LSW, and Tricia Ryden, PhD, for their thoughtful, wise and helpful observations and suggestions as we developed this story. ♥

The Peace of Mind Program, developed by author Linda Ryden and shared by the nonprofit organization Peace of Mind Inc, teaches children to notice and manage their emotions, build healthy relationships, solve conflicts peacefully, and stand up to injustice. The Peace of Mind Program includes a mindfulness-based social emotional learning curriculum for Early Childhood through Middle School, training and support for educators, and a nation-wide community of practice.

TeachPeaceofMind.org

Peace of Mind Inc., Washington, D.C. 20015
https://TeachPeaceofMind.org
Copyright 2022 Peace of Mind Inc.

Peace of Mind is a registered trademark of Peace of Mind Inc. All rights reserved. NO part of this book may be reproduced, storied in a retrieval system, or transmitted by any means, electronic or otherwise, without prior written permission from the author.

Cover and interior design: Schwa Design Group
Library of Congress Control Number: 2022916612
ISBN 978-1-7373423-5-9
Published 2022

Printed in the USA
CPSIA information can be obtained
at www.ICGtesting.com
LVHW071154131123
763661LV00017B/865

9 781737 342359